A Taste of
Chicken Soup for the Soul®

Food
and Love

Stories Celebrating Special Times with
Family and Friends ... and Recipes Too!

Jack Canfield

Mark Victor Hansen

Amy Newmark

Chicken Soup for the Soul Publishing, LLC
Cos Cob, CT

A Taste of Chicken Soup for the Soul: Food and Love
Stories Celebrating Special Times with Family and Friends
... and Recipes Too!
Jack Canfield, Mark Victor Hansen and Amy Newmark

Published by Chicken Soup for the Soul Publishing, LLC

www.chickensoup.com

Front cover photo courtesy of iStockphoto.com/fertnig (© Chris Fertnig)

Library of Congress Control Number: 2011937663

A Taste of ISBN: 978-1-61159-867-4

Full Book ISBN: 978-1-935096-78-8

Contents

Becoming a Cook

Cooking is like love. It should be entered
into with abandon or not at all.
~Harriet van Horne

"Do you like Hamburger Helper?" my soon-to-be-husband's twelve-year-old son, Austin, asked me the first time I met him. "I hope so because it's the only thing my dad knows how to cook."

"It's okay, honey, I can cook," I assured him without even thinking.

He eyed me suspiciously. "What do you know how to make?"

I shrugged and then plunged into the abyss of deception. "I know how to cook lots of things. What do you like to eat?"

He shrugged back. "I like pretty much

everything. Well, except Hamburger Helper."
He wrinkled his nose. "I'm kind of tired of
that."

I laughed. "If you like pretty much everything, we should be just fine in the food
department."

He grinned and looked at his dad. "Marry
her tomorrow, Dad. Seriously."

Eric and I followed Austin's suggestion and
got married just five months after we met. I
quit my job and moved the two hundred miles
from my apartment in the Chicago suburbs to
Eric's farmhouse in southern Indiana. His kids
and my kids got along the way blood siblings
do—loving each other one minute and fighting
the next. And Eric, well, he was practically perfect in the husband department. Things were
going exactly according to plan.

Except for one thing. That little white lie I'd
told. I'd said I could cook. Talk about the mother
of all exaggerations! Yeah, I can cook—if calling
the pizza delivery boy qualifies as cooking! Saying I could cook was like saying I could fly. It

hadn't happened yet, but who knew? But maybe I could figure it out and then I'd never have to fess up to my little fabrication.

The pressure was on. I could practically hear Rachael Ray's voice taunting me, "Did you tell that poor kid you know how to cook? How could you do such a thing?"

But Emeril, the angel on my other shoulder, responded, "It's all right. She'll learn." And then he added a "Bam!" just to encourage me.

For the first few months, I faked it with easy stuff like spaghetti and tacos. We grilled hamburgers and brats on the grill at least once a week. It was summer, so nobody expected me to spend a lot of time in the kitchen. But I knew winter was coming and that meant the grill—my new best friend—would soon be going into hibernation.

I panicked, but not for long. I soon found a new favorite appliance—my crock pot. You can throw practically anything in that thing and it turns out all right. At first, I made sure I had a recipe and I followed it exactly. But after a while, I got creative and started throwing in whatever I had on hand. One day, I tossed in some boneless, skinless chicken breasts, a packet of onion soup mix, and a can of cream-of-whatever soup.

When Eric got home from work, he took a bite of my creation, which I'd mixed with egg noodles. His eyebrows went up and he nodded. "This is pretty good. What's it called?"

"Um, let me check," I said. I reached for a cookbook, flipped through to the section of chicken recipes and read the first one I saw. "Perfect Breasts," I said.

Eric grinned. "Excellent. Be sure to make this one again. Maybe just for me next time." He wiggled his eyebrows suggestively.

Chalk one up for me and my "cooking" skills.

After I mastered my crock pot, I discovered some really great cooking websites. One site's specialty was recipes that required just five ingredients.

Even I couldn't mess that up. I printed

some of the more appealing ones and tried them out. They were really good. Even my oh-so-picky daughters asked for seconds.

I was getting pretty good at faking the cooking thing.

And then the real test came: my husband's birthday. In his family, birthdays are a huge deal. The whole family comes over to celebrate, but no one serves just cake and ice cream. No, these people come hungry and ready for a good, home-cooked meal.

Did I mention my husband is one of eight children?

Yeah, so about forty people—including my new mother-in-law—came over to our house, expecting food that was not only edible, but actually tasty. I was beyond overwhelmed by it all.

I filled two crock pots with chicken, boiled some egg noodles, fixed some bread—the kind that comes in the tubes—heated about a dozen cans of green beans, and hoped for the best. If the food were terrible, there would always be cake. It was store-bought, so I couldn't mess it up.

I watched closely as my mother-in-law took her first bite of the chicken I'd made. Her eyes lit up and she quickly took another bite.

Holy cow, she liked it. I had pulled it off after all.

When my husband's sister asked me for the recipe, I picked up my jaw from the floor and stammered, "Oh, you don't want this recipe. It's so easy, it's embarrassing."

She smiled. "But those are the best kinds of recipes."

I rattled off the five-ingredient recipe, ashamed that now everyone would peg me for the fake I was.

"Diane, that chicken was delicious," another sister-in-law said. "The fact that it was easy to cook only makes me like it more."

"But I'm really not a very good cook," I insisted.

"Did you make the meal today?" my mother-in-law asked.

"Well, yeah," I said.

"Then you're a good cook."

I looked into the smiling faces of the women in my new family. And I realized that becoming a good cook was a lot like becoming a member of their family.

It didn't matter how I'd gotten there. But I was sure glad I finally had.

Cream Cheese Chicken

4 boneless skinless chicken breasts
½ cup butter
1 package Italian seasoning mix
1 (8 oz.) package cream cheese
1 (10¾ oz.) can cream of chicken soup
Cooked rice or pasta

Cube chicken into bite-sized pieces.

Combine chicken pieces, butter and Italian

seasoning mix in a Crock-Pot (slow cooker) and cook on low for 6 to 8 hours.

Then add cream cheese and soup, and cook on high until cheese is melted.

Serve over rice or pasta.

~*Diane Stark*

The Inside Story

I was 32 when I started cooking;
up until then, I just ate.
~Julia Child

I stared at the chicken section in the grocery store, trying to figure out why there were so many options. There were legs, thighs, whole organic chickens, split breasts, breasts with skins, skinless breasts, fryer chickens and roaster chickens. The choices seemed endless. At least I knew I wanted to make a whole chicken. But which one? Should it be the fryer or the roaster?

I had never cooked a chicken before in my life. I had just moved into my new home with the man of my dreams and I had a baby on the way. The tears started stinging my eyes. My only option was to pick up my cell phone and call my mom. I told her where I was and what my great dilemma was. There was a familiar sound on the other end of the phone. Still staring at the chicken choices in front of me I sighed, "Mom, are you laughing at me?"

I believe she hiccupped and erupted into another fit of hysterics. At that point I hung up. Yes, I hung up on my mother. Here I was, young and ambitious, willing to showcase my love for my family through food, and the chicken was defeating me. And all my mother could do was laugh at me? I almost stormed out of the grocery store and ordered pizza for dinner.

Instead, I called her back, "Are you done yet?"

Gasping for breath she replied, "Yes," and then started laughing again.

I stood in front of all that chicken while my mom tried to catch her breath and I struggled with the great chicken debate.

"You... should... get... a... roaster..." she

replied between gasps of breath.

"Thank you, Mom," I said, with an attitude that said I wasn't playing around, and hung up.

I grabbed my roaster chicken, paid for my other groceries and went home. I took the chicken out, grabbed a pan, gathered some spices and was getting ready to cook that bad boy up when my phone rang.

"Yes?" I said.

It was my mom again. She had taken control of herself.

"Are you cooking the chicken?" she asked.

"Yes," I said.

"Did you take the innards out?" she said softly.

"The what?" I pulled the phone away from my ear and stared at it like she could see me.

When I put the phone back to my ear she was saying, "...inside the chicken. You have to take that stuff out."

I looked at the chicken. I saw the little opening where its head used to be. "I'm not sticking my hand in that."

She snickered into the phone, "Oh yes you are, if you're cooking that chicken and not trying to kill anyone. You need to take the plastic bag with the innards out before you cook it."

I believe at that point I made a sound that was something akin to, "blechhhgrossill-ick-ick-ick!"

My mom's voice went soft in my ear. "I'll tell you a story while you take the insides of the chicken out."

"Okay, I'm listening," I said while having an internal conflict about sticking my hand inside the chicken.

"I didn't always know how to cook." I could hear the smile and whimsy in her voice. "And, I can still remember the first meatloaf I tried to cook for your father. I was so young. All I wanted to do was make a home-cooked meal for my family. So I gathered all my ingredients, mixed up that meat, added eggs, breadcrumbs, seasoning and then I flattened it as I put it in the pan."

"Why?" I might not have been the best cook around but I had never heard of flattening a meatloaf.

"Well, my dear, I thought that my meatloaf would rise in the oven just like bread rises. It turns out, it doesn't."

"You didn't!"

"I did. I'll never forget that meatloaf. Just like you'll never forget your chicken. Did you get the insides out?"

I had not noticed but I was holding a dripping bag filled with neck, liver and who knows what else in my free hand. I had just plunged my hand right in, grabbed that bag and pulled it out while my mom told me her story.

"Yes, I got it," I said into the phone.

"Just throw them away for now. I'll tell you how to use them on your next chicken," she said with a slight hitch in her voice. I think she was about to laugh again.

"Thanks, Mom," I said, and suddenly I was reassured that it was okay. It didn't matter if my chicken didn't come out perfect or if my mother's meatloaf never rose. It only mattered that I wanted to do something for my family and was making the effort to do it. That was the whole concept of food and love that my mother had taught me growing up.

"Don't forget to give the chicken a good butter massage before putting your spices on it," she said and hung up.

"What?" Wasn't sticking my hand inside it enough? Now I had to give the bird a spa treatment before eating it. I was never going to cook a chicken again. Never. Ever.

It has been ten years since my first chicken. I've grown quite experienced in the art of cooking a chicken. I have cooked hundreds of chickens over the years—some fryers, some roasters, each one better than the last. I'm no longer grossed out about sticking my hand inside a bird or having to feel it up before cooking it to a tender juicy crisp. And, I know that one day I'm going to have to tell my son the story of the first chicken I tried to cook for his father when he calls me up to complain that my future daughter-in-law doesn't know the difference between halibut and flounder. I may have to tell him about Grandma's meat-loaf too.

~*Linda St.Cyr*

And So I Made Soup

There is nothing like a plate or a bowl
of hot soup, its wisp of aromatic steam making
the nostrils quiver with anticipation, to dispel the
depressing effects of a grueling day at the office
or the shop, rain or snow in the streets,
or bad news in the papers.
~*Louis P. De Gouy*, The Soup Book

We'd been treating David's follow-up appointments as dates—first seeing the doctor, then sharing lunch and shopping afterwards. After all, with four of our eight children still living at home, time alone together was always at a premium. But on that particular day our eight-year-old daughter Katie seemed to need some one-on-one attention, so we'd brought her along.

While I'd always been in the exam room as

the doctor checked inside my husband's throat, this time I stayed in the waiting room with Katie. I wasn't sure she could handle the sight of the doctor putting tubes down her father's nose. She and I talked animatedly until I fell silent after a good half hour had passed. I was starting to get nervous. These check-ups usually lasted less than twenty minutes.

After forty-five minutes, I got a sick feeling in the pit of my stomach. As my daughter read a book she'd brought, I clutched my hands, silently praying for my husband. Fifteen minutes later, when the nurse came out and said the doctor wanted to speak to me, I already knew why. When I entered the exam room I first glanced at the doctor's serious expression, then David's ashen complexion.

"Is it back?" I asked, and David nodded. My stomach lurched, and I felt like throwing up.

On the screen that showed the inside of my husband's throat, the doctor pointed out a growth on the epiglottis and said he was ninety-nine percent certain it was cancer. In the stunned quiet of the room, I thought I heard the unmistakable sound of the other shoe dropping.

It had been less than two years since my spouse had faced a diagnosis of oral cancer and undergone an invasive surgery that left him with a tracheotomy and a feeding tube. Surgery had been followed by a grueling six-week regimen of radiation and chemotherapy.

The day after the doctor's pronouncement that the cancer had likely returned, our son Dan found me in the kitchen, stirring two huge pots of homemade soup. The table was littered with more than a dozen single serving containers that I ladled soup into for storing in the freezer. Dan didn't even have to ask me why I was making mass quantities of soup, he instinctively knew. You see, he and I had been down this road already, a team united in support of his dad. Two years before, when I'd become David's caregiver, Dan had been a crucial support for both of us. He'd put his own life on hold to run errands, visit David daily in the hospital for an eleven-day stretch, and take him to appointments. He basically became a rock for me to lean on.

Dan knew exactly why I was making soup. It was one of the few things I could do. Despite our best intentions in providing a support system for David, in the end, cancer is a lonely fight. It would be David who would have to experience another surgery and additional chemotherapy, David who would be fighting for his life. I could hardly bear the thought.

So I made soup.

David hadn't been able to eat at all after his surgery. I'd fed him liquid food through a tube in his abdomen, gradually introducing soft foods. Foods like soup. Then during radiation and chemotherapy treatments, with his throat raw and sore, soup was the one food he could still manage to swallow. Even after his recovery from treatment his throat was narrowed, swollen with scar tissue. Soup remained the single food he could consume without coughing or choking. When we went out to eat, the soup of the day was the first thing he asked about. I'd gotten lazy, though, relying on canned soups. Making homemade soup was a tangible way to show David I would be there for him, whatever lay ahead. Homemade soup was love.

When the doctor's office called a week later to report that the surgical biopsy was benign, I got to experience the heady feeling people must have when they win the lottery. For months afterward, each time I pulled a single serving of soup from the freezer, I was reminded of our good fortune. With my husband waiting patiently at the table, I'd pop the container in the microwave and serve it piping hot with little oyster crackers floating on top. Then I'd kiss the top of David's head as I served it, silently thanking God for the blessing of my husband.

That was three years ago. David is now a five-year cancer survivor and our marriage is the best it has ever been. The few times that we have disagreed or exchanged harsh words I have made sure to dredge up the memories of that fateful doctor's appointment when we were certain that David's cancer had returned.

Then I head to the stove to make soup.

Mary's Oven Stew

2 lb. stew meat
6–8 potatoes, peeled and cubed
6 carrots, sliced
½ cup chopped celery
1 large can of tomato juice and 1 small can of beef broth
1 bag frozen peas
1 bag frozen corn
2 tablespoons minced onion or chopped onion, to taste
pepper to taste

Mix all ingredients except for corn and peas in a roasting pan.

Cook for 4 hours at 200 degrees.

Add 1 bag frozen corn, 1 bag frozen peas.

Cook another hour.

~*Mary Potter Kenyon*

Life, Remodeled

It takes a long time to grow an old friend.
~John Leonard

I made the first phone calls in July, attempting to reunite five old friends for dinner. We had been close during our somewhat carefree and unfettered young adulthood. Now in our sixties, we were balancing medical dilemmas and late career issues with grandparenting duties and other long-awaited pleasures. Finding common availability was a challenge. I functioned like a general contractor trying to coordinate the plumber, electrician, carpenter, and painter to arrive in perfect sequence. We finally set a date for the second Saturday in October. It was worth the effort—these are memory-rich relationships. It was also worth the wait—I hadn't spent an entire evening with these folks in over twenty-five years. A lot had changed.

Though I don't see these friends often, I nurture an emotional connection with them. We met in our early twenties, married from the same small pool, and remained close through our children's grade school years. But circumstance pushed us in different directions, and we found fewer and fewer opportunities to be together.

With a date on the calendar at last, eager to begin planning our dinner I leafed through recipes to determine a menu. The meal had to be luscious, healthy, and uncomplicated to prepare and serve. Mike and I did not want to spend most of the evening in aprons, conversing with our guests while juggling whisks and wooden spoons. I polled a trio of girlfriends for ideas.

"Pork roast," recommended one. "Just be really careful not to overcook it," she said.

"Red potatoes," said another, "basted in a blend of lemon juice and rosemary garlic butter every fifteen minutes while they bake, then sprinkled with lemon zest just before they're done. But watch out," she cautioned. "It's easy to forget to add that grated lemon peel while you're visiting with your company."

"A baked root vegetable dish is great this time of year," suggested the third. "And it can be slid into the oven and almost ignored. And oh, hot garlic bread would be perfect."

How big do these people think my oven is?

Finally, I came up with a menu Mike and I could manage and still feel like we'd be part of the party and not a catering team. A salad of romaine lettuce, apple slices, dried cranberries, and Gorgonzola tossed with lime-cumin dressing. A warm loaf of ciabatta. Chicken breasts marinated in seasoned buttermilk and baked in a toasted sesame seed and breadcrumb crust. Orzo cooked in buttery chicken broth. Steamed green beans tossed with olive oil and chopped cashews. And for dessert, pumpkin pie custard topped with a crust of rich buttered crumbs and finished with whipped cream.

Some years back, these friends had spent so much time in my house they could have navigated the main floor blindfolded. But time passed quicker than the shelf life of a cream puff, and suddenly they hadn't been over for decades. So the weekend before our party, Mike and I cleaned from basement to attic in case they asked for a tour of the house's updates or just a hike down memory lane. I wanted to be prepared for whatever the evening would serve us.

Since their last visit the kitchen had been remodeled, and the only feature they'd recognize would be the curve of window seats and the round table they had routinely crowded around in years past. I hoped they'd like the bright whiteness of the room, and feel warmed by the golden oak floor. Room by room, contemporary furniture situated on luminous hardwood replaced what they'd known. I converted to the Tao of minimalism fifteen years ago, and tossed out the tchotchkes with which they were familiar. Gone were the trappings of raising children. Would they miss the comfort of that "lived in" look?

Outside, a graceful river birch thrived where the old maple lived and died, and we had recently planted a crab apple to shade the front door. The mature arborvitae trees that bookended the house had grown gangly and Mike removed them a few years ago. Recently added dormers perched on the roof might disorient our visitors if the landscaping didn't. I reminded myself to have the front light fixed so our guests could read our address if they were thrown off by the unfamiliar. A lot of the recognizable features of the house were gone, both inside and out, but I anticipated approval by these venerable comrades.

The most significant update my friends would notice was that I had installed a new husband. This would not surprise them, since they'd all met Mike briefly at the occasional wedding, funeral, or chance encounter at the movies. But none of them actually knew him.

They'd soon observe that he was quite different from my former spouse. Two of them went to college with Husband Number One and still join him for a few rounds of golf every summer.

October tenth arrived. Candles were lit and the food almost ready when we opened the front door to our visitors. Roasting chicken seasoned with rosemary and thyme scented the air. The windows were fogged by steam from simmering green beans and pasta. Our guests squeezed into the window seats around the kitchen table just as they used to, while Mike tossed salad at the counter. As I darted between the microwave, refrigerator, and stove, I enjoyed hearing his laughter blend into the happy cacophony of long-familiar voices.

We filled our salad plates and moved into the dining room. The conversation jumped from nostalgia to hilarious nonsense to contemplation, and never lagged. My friends regaled Mike with adventures from the past that cast me in a far more charming light than

I remember. We toasted the past and hailed the future.

Near midnight, we pushed ourselves out from the table and rose on stiffened legs. We reveled in a prolonged ritual of fond kisses and lingering hugs mingled with laughter. Our company trooped out and Mike closed the front door.

"I had fun getting to know your buddies," he said. I grinned and gave him a kiss.

"Thanks for being you," I replied, satisfied with the simplicity of the compliment. After we loaded and started the dishwasher we then climbed the stairs, leaving that humming and whirring beast alone in the dark to do its dirty work. I felt half exhilarated, half exhausted.

Once we snuggled into bed, Mike chortled and teased about the fresh rendering he'd seen of me in my younger years. After he dozed off I lay still and happy, reflecting. My friends had seen my current reality. They saw the changes I'd made to my house and to my life over these past few decades. Lots of bricks were shuffled around. Some were removed. I knew they liked my modifications, great and small, and that they still liked me.

I breathed in the same air my husband exhaled. Content, I closed my eyes under the protective roof of this sound home.

~Beverly A. Golberg

Battered Love

I love being married. It's so great to find
that one special person you want to annoy
for the rest of your life.
~Rita Rudner

"Buy this. Buy this." My husband hollered from the far end of the grocery aisle. In his arms he carried a huge blue bag of something. I couldn't tell what it was from a distance.

Since retiring, filling his day with a variety of activities turned out to be a challenge for Richard. That morning he'd decided we'd spend the day at the local warehouse club. He'd convinced me that I would get in my daily exercise by walking through and browsing the many products in the oversized store.

As Richard approached, I discovered he was carrying a plastic re-sealable ten-pound bag of buttermilk pancake mix.

"What the heck are you going to do with that?" I asked.

"What do you think I'm going to do with it? Make pancakes." He heaved it into the basket, narrowly missing the eggs.

I leaned into the cart to read the label on the back of the bag. "This makes 250 pancakes. Are you crazy?"

"Breakfast for nine cents a day. We're retired, remember?" was his retort. "I have to save us money any way I can."

"But that's enough for a Kiwanis Club all you can eat pancake breakfast. We'll never be able to eat all that," I replied.

Richard's eyes had that glazed over look that meant he wasn't listening to me at all. "That's not a bad idea. Maybe I'll get two bags. You love pancakes, don't you?"

I didn't answer. Actually I preferred a bowl of hot oatmeal for breakfast. I liked to stir in a big glob of creamy peanut butter and then top it off with my favorite, strawberries, kind of like a peanut butter and jelly sandwich. I'm a creature of habit and wasn't in any hurry to change my routine just to save a few pennies.

"It's only 140 calories for two pancakes. I'm saving you money and watching your weight." Richard raced off to the next aisle to see what other bargains he could find.

A few days later I spotted the big blue bag sitting on the kitchen counter. Without being told, I knew Richard's activity for today would involve cooking the cheap, low-calorie pancakes.

I watched him carefully measure out the mix. He slowly poured in the water as he stirred the batter with an oversized wire whisk. Dry pancake mix puffed out of the bowl with each dip of the utensil. Soon white powder coated his face and chest.

The batter sputtered as it hit the hot frying pan. When the pancakes began to bubble, Richard flipped them and they sputtered again. Stacks of golden brown circles began to form on plates sitting on the counter. As soon as one pancake made its way onto the cooling stack, more batter made its way into the pan.

"Do you have to make so many?" I asked.

"If I'm going to charge five dollars a plate, I need to practice." He grinned and winked.

Humming a tune, Richard settled into an easy rhythm of stirring, pouring and flipping. The piles of pancakes grew so tall they leaned to one side. I tried to resist when my mouth began to water as the aroma of breakfast filled the house. Maybe I would like this after all.

A few minutes later I heard the burners on the stove click off. I saw two boxes of Ziploc bags come out of the drawer.

"I need help," Richard called out. "Two pancakes in a small bag. Ten small bags in a big bag."

"Cooking pancakes is awfully messy. Do you really think it's worth it?" I curled up my nose in disgust at the sight of the dirty kitchen.

"You're going to love them, you wait and see," he said as I stuffed pancakes into a sandwich-sized bag. "It's all about the portion control. Only take out of the freezer what you need. Every morning, ready-made pancakes in a minute."

"How long will it take us to eat all these?" I asked.

"When we run out, I'll make some more. I still have half a bag of mix left."

I cringed. "You're enjoying this, aren't you?"

"I should have been a short order cook." He blew me a powdery kiss. "Just wait until you taste my pancakes."

Richard glowed from head to toe, not from the dust or the dots of creamy batter on his shirt, but from the inside out. I should have found the pride he displayed in his accomplishment and the freezer full of pancakes contagious. Except for the fact that I was hooked on my version of breakfast comfort food, not his.

With Richard occupied in the kitchen, the only thing I could think of was oatmeal. Oatmeal with peanut butter. Two minutes in the microwave, one dish to clean up, and a full stomach all morning. It was only a matter of time before pancakes encroached on my morning routine.

A few days later, I noticed that some ready-made pancakes had made their way to the refrigerator to thaw. Twenty pancakes. Breakfast for us both for a week.

"I'm making breakfast this morning," he announced. "Go read the paper."

Still in my nightgown, I curled up on the sofa. I woke up with my heart set on a high fat scoop of peanut butter swirled into my cholesterol-reducing oatmeal, my morning guilty pleasure. In a matter of minutes a warm plate of pancakes topped with syrup, butter and fresh strawberries found its way onto my lap.

Still skeptical I held the plate under my nose, breathing in. The food smelled divine. Then I smeared around the little dabs of butter with my fork, licking the utensil clean. I cut off a tiny piece of pancake and speared it along with a strawberry. Swirling the forkful in a pool of syrup I slowly raised it to my mouth.

I savored the sweetness of the hot golden circles. "Mmmm. This is delicious." The taste surprised me, sweet, creamy, sticky, kind of like my oatmeal only not so lumpy. "I think I could get used to this."

"We have a freezer full. You can have pancakes every day if you want," he replied.

I devoured every last morsel on the plate. "Is there more?" I asked holding my empty plate out for Richard to see. "I think you might have won me over."

Richard's eyes sparkled back at me. He put another pancake on my plate and placed it in the microwave. While it warmed up he reached into the cupboard and pulled out a canister of oatmeal.

"Can I throw this away?" He waved the box in my direction.

"What will I eat when we run out of pancakes?"

"Don't worry. We won't," he answered.

He set down the plate of seconds on the

counter in front of me. As I took a bite, I knew we would never run out. Pancakes had made us both happy, satisfied, fulfilled, and indulged. Richard had won me over after all.

~Linda C. Wright

A Blast from the Past

Pleasure is the flower that passes;
remembrance, the lasting perfume.
~Jean de Boufflers

Recently I went to lunch at a small neighborhood deli that serves a variety of sandwiches on healthy breads. On the counter at the cash register there was an assortment of not-so-healthy homemade cakes sectioned into thick squares, displayed in clear plastic containers with handwritten labels. My mouth watered at the sight of a chunk of carrot cake. I flirted with a chocolate-frosted wedge, but then my heart skipped a beat as I recognized a long-lost love. Memories flooded back from more than thirty years ago and I gave in to that scrumptious chunk of apple walnut cake. I devoured every tasty morsel, even the crumbs sticking to the plastic container.

I sat at a retro wooden table, similar to the one in my friend's old kitchen, to eat my lunch. Every forkful of that apple walnut cake resurrected happy memories of my late friend and our dearly departed mothers. Rose and I were best friends and next-door neighbors for ten years. We had the same warped sense of humor. We shared coffee and sweets, gossip and good news. We cried on one another's shoulders, complained about our spouses and shared child-rearing tips. We parented our parents too—like most women of that generation, we took care of everybody else's needs first.

When we had a little time to ourselves, we would sit in Rose's kitchen as she baked desserts that rivaled those sold at the neighborhood bakery. Her banana cream cake was spectacular and her brownies decadent. But the apple walnut cake, with its cinnamon goodness, had just the right combination of smooth, moist, coffee cake texture, crunchy nuts and fresh fruit. We decided it was a healthy dessert and nibbled on it for days, sliver by sliver, trying to make it last. It was one of our simple indulgences.

Rose and I chauffeured our moms to grocery stores and bingo halls, and we also took them on leisurely Sunday drives. One fall day, they invited us to accompany them on a day trip with the senior citizen group. An old-fashioned picnic with apple picking sounded like something we would enjoy, so we boarded the chartered bus along with our mothers and forty other senior citizens. Rose and I seated our moms up front and then sat across the aisle from one another further back. Bits and pieces of conversations floated our way. We overheard one word repeatedly—nurses. When several ladies stopped to ask what malady our moms suffered from, since obviously they needed their nurses along, we chuckled and explained our relationships.

At the picnic grounds, the seniors lined up to receive their boxed lunches. Rose and I darted to the restroom. As we were heading back, we both gasped at the sight of our moms. We realized that we were too far away to prevent the inevitable from occurring. We sprinted towards them but could only watch as they lifted one leg and then the other over the old-fashioned, wooden picnic bench and placed their open boxes on the table. Simultaneously they sat down. On the same side of the bench! One end of the small picnic table seesawed up in the air as our moms flopped backwards onto the grassy ground. Their milk splashed them, their apples rolled down the hill and their ham sandwiches ended up in the dirt. By the time we reached our wide-eyed moms, lying flat on their backs with their feet in the air, flustered from the tumble, all we could do was laugh. We regained our composure and helped them up. We apologized for laughing and gave them our boxed lunches.

On the bus ride home, Rose and I couldn't look at each other without giggling. As a diversion, we counted the apples in our bags and we stared out the windows until one of us caught a glimpse of the other in the reflection. We tried to stifle chuckles and snorts, guffaws and snickers. We were a mess. We took our moms home, thanked them for a memorable day and made sure they were okay. Then we laughed all the way to Rose's kitchen. We peeled and chopped our newly picked apples and made another delicious apple walnut cake.

Over the years, there were many times Rose and I sat in her kitchen and shared tidbits of our lives as we devoured delicious home-baked goods. None was ever sweeter than that particular apple walnut coffee cake.

Apple Walnut Coffee Cake

Beat together:
1½ cups vegetable oil
2 cups granulated sugar
2 eggs

Sift together:
3 cups flour
1 teaspoon baking soda
2 teaspoons cinnamon (more to taste)
2 teaspoons vanilla

Mix all ingredients

Peel and dice 3 heaping cups apples

Fold in apples

Add 1 cup chopped walnuts

Bake at 350 degrees for 1 hour in greased and floured 9x13 pan.

Cool and dust with powdered sugar

~Linda O'Connell

Food Served with Love Tastes Best

There is no greater loan than a sympathetic ear.
~Frank Tyger

"Your mouth looks like chopped liver," the dentist said. "You have three cavities!"

No wonder I had such a toothache. I felt so ashamed. It must have been all those chocolate chip cookies I ate as my dinner. Most days I'd buy a box on my way home from work, along with a paperback mystery—my way of escaping into oblivion. At twenty-three, I was miserable, working at a job I hated, unhappily single while my two best friends were married.

In 1965, "nice girls" lived at home until they married. But the four-bedroom apartment in the Bronx where I lived with my parents was suffocating. It was the sixties, and times were changing. Young singles flocked to Manhattan to work and play.

"Everyone's moving to the city now!" I told my mother.

"So if everyone jumped off the Brooklyn Bridge, would you?" she asked.

I daydreamed about a glamorous life in the city. I'd go to folk concerts, throw wild parties, have fun! But when I actually moved into a studio apartment in Manhattan, my life often felt empty.

To pay the rent, I worked at a state agency, helping men on parole find jobs. Young and inexperienced, I was terrified by those rough guys who'd served time for armed robbery, murder and dealing drugs.

Weekends were daunting. At best there'd be a dinner date, but long stretches of empty time made me ache for someone to love. One evening at a dance, in the arms of a stranger, I feared I'd be alone forever, going to work, and then numbing myself with mystery novels and junk food. I couldn't bear to marry until I was in love, but how long would I have to wait?

When the phone rang, it was often my mother, worrying about me.

"Have you met anyone yet? Are you getting out to socialize? Did you hear that Harriet is engaged to a doctor?" Her barrage of questions made me feel like a total failure.

The worst blues hit on Sunday nights, when I pictured everyone else nesting with their loved ones. That's when I'd pick up the phone and call my Aunt Libby to see if she was home for a visit.

My mother's younger sister, Libby, had never married. Feisty and independent, she was the only woman in my family with a career. As secretary to New York's traffic commissioner, she rode to work in a limousine! Even without a husband or children, she seemed way happier than my mother. Watching her live with zest made me feel less anxious about being single.

On those Sunday nights, I walked down Lexington Avenue, past the florist with lilacs

in the window, past the Mom and Pop sta-
tionery store, then down the steps to the dingy
subway. As the train rumbled along, I daydreamed about seeing Aunt Libby again.

I pressed the bell to her apartment, she
buzzed me into the building, and I could
hardly wait for the elevator to take me to the
fifth floor. There she stood at the end of the hall
in the open doorway, beaming at me—a tall,
zaftig woman with curly hair, her dark eyes
shining with love.

When she enveloped me in a comforting
hug, happiness flooded me. I inhaled the
lemon scent of her cologne, absorbed her
warmth, and knew everything in my life was
going to be all right.

Inside the apartment, Libby settled on the
loveseat, while I plopped down on the antique
oak rocking chair with a blue Chinese rug at
its feet. Healthy houseplants in brass pots and
oak floors polished to a gleam made the apartment a welcoming home.

After a while, we entered the narrow

kitchen where Libby made our tuna supper. It was simple, yet wonderful. Tuna mashed up with plenty of mayonnaise and diced onion. Juicy tomato wedges. Potato salad fixed with mayonnaise, grated carrots and celery. Some slices of soft challah—a braided egg bread with a glossy brown crust that tasted almost as sweet as cake.

As we ate, we talked about everyday things. Libby's friend Dora, who was fighting with her husband. My horrible boss, a skinny man with a beak for a nose, who ordered me to wear suits. My latest boyfriend, or lack of one.

"I don't know what you see in Gino," Libby said. "He's so coarse!"

She meant my Italian boyfriend, a printer with fingernails permanently stained with ink. He spoke like Marlon Brando in *On the Waterfront*. To me, he was tough and sexy, so exotic compared to the nice Jewish men I grew up with. Still, Libby's comment stopped me from considering him as "husband material."

What I remember most is our laughter; Libby laughing so hard tears ran down her cheeks, me laughing until I could hardly breathe. She got hysterical about the time I flushed her ring down the toilet when I was two years old.

"I still owe you a ring," I said.

"You're off the hook." She held out a gold ring she'd found on the street, a piece of good luck proving life was full of wonderful surprises. When she died she left it to me, along with her mother's diamond ring.

Tears of sorrow flooded Libby's eyes when told me how much she missed her mother. Libby was free with her joys and open with her sorrows. Everything between us flowed easily. In Libby's apartment I could be myself without worrying about what I said.

One night, as we sipped tea and nibbled on macaroons, I confessed I was dropping out of my master's program in English Literature.

"I made such a mistake, wasting a year and all that money. I should finish, but I just don't want to!" I agonized.

"That's why they made erasers," Libby said, brushing away my regrets. What a relief! Libby made me see that mistakes were human. I could change my path and start over.

Just hearing her name still evokes a feeling of home. She's passed on, but her tuna suppers live on in my life, reminding me of her loving spirit. My husband Tom and I fix those suppers here in Portland on Sunday nights, in memory of Libby, and to share a quiet evening of our own.

Together we prepare the tuna. Tom mashes it until it has a flaky texture; I add mayonnaise and salty capers. Like Libby, I arrange tomato wedges along with some new touches: carrot sticks, green olives, sweet pickles, and celery stuffed with cheese.

"I love our Sunday night suppers," Tom said recently. We were snuggled up together on the couch, after a tuna supper, watching a movie.

"Yes, they're so comforting," I said.

When I fix food to share with someone I love, no matter how simple the meal, it feeds my soul. Tuna suppers have become a beloved ritual in our home, and I always feel thankful to Aunt Libby for that tradition, and for the comfort she gave me years ago.

~Barbara Blossom Ashmun

Tough Love in the Kitchen

Children have to be educated, but they have
also to be left to educate themselves.
~Abbé Dimnet

"I'm staging a cooking strike," I said to my husband when he came through the door from work.

"The kids must be complaining again about all the 'yucky' food you've been cooking." He smiled wryly.

"That's exactly what's happened. Brian asked me to start making smooth 'white' applesauce like they serve at school. Holly wants me to start buying corn that comes in a can. The whole thing blew up for me today at lunch when our junior food critics said the pizza crust was a 'bit too done.' The only thing that's overdone in this house is me!" I lamented.

"Why don't you just tell them you cook to please me and not them?" he asked with a sigh.

"We've used that strategy before and it goes in one ear and out the other," I said. The kids' grousing had created needless mealtime disruptions turning what should be quality family time into a not-so-pleasant dinnertime discourse.

My husband could tell I'd made up my mind to address the problem head on. "You're right; a cooking strike might make them more appreciative of what it takes to prepare meals. So what's the plan and how are we going to implement it?"

Our family was fortunate that I was able to be a full-time stay-at-home mom who loved cooking and baking. We lived on a small farm in Washington State where we raised all our own meat and poultry. Every year we planted a huge vegetable garden, with adjoining blueberry and raspberry patches framed by apple and plum trees. The food was wholesome and plentiful.

My kids, just nine and eleven years old, didn't look at it quite the same way. Their continual fault finding sent a message that what I cooked for them was substandard. The truth was, they didn't know any different, as they'd grown up with nothing other than home cooking and baking made from quality ingredients.

That night, after a thoroughly scrutinized meal of parmesan meatloaf, mashed potatoes and fresh corn and peas from our garden, we told the kids we wanted to have a family discussion in the living room.

"First thing Saturday morning a cooking strike will begin in our house, which means you two are on your own for cooking and preparing all of your own meals," I explained to them.

"Why aren't you going to cook, Mom?" Brian asked.

"You two have been bellyaching about everything I cook for months on end, so it's time to see if you can do a better job for yourselves. You've had more than your share of warnings that I was going to take some action toward ending the complaining and this is it. We'll stock the pantry shelves and the refrigerator with foods you can eat cold, along with some homemade TV dinners for you to just pop into the microwave. Holly, you can manage easy things on the stove like toasted cheese or egg sandwiches and soup.

"The rules are easy: inform either me or Dad if you're going to use the stove; you eat what you cook; and all the dishes need to be cleaned up every time you use the kitchen," I instructed.

"Do you both understand what's going on here and why?" their dad asked.

"I guess so," Holly replied softly. "Dad, how long is the strike going to last?"

"We have to see how things go, but the length of the strike is your mother's call." She and her brother exchanged unsure glances.

The plan was in place and it couldn't have been more perfect!

The mood was light during the first week.

The budding chefs weren't taking the strike seriously—it was still a game. I heard a lot of giggling and whispering coming from the kitchen. They teamed up to help each other learn more about using the microwave, and they were good sports about sharing the choice foods.

Grumbling began at the start of week two. I overheard Holly ask Brian if he wanted a fried bologna sandwich, to which he replied, "Oh, not another fried bologna sandwich!"

By the end of the second week there was moaning about having to eat the food they made. They expressed concern about their dwindling supply of provisions, particularly graham crackers and vanilla wafers.

In the first days of week three they started turning on the charm and began enlisting me to cross the picket line to teach them some cooking tips. They were silently hoping at any moment I'd surrender the cause by waving a white apron overhead and prepare a meal that none of us would ever forget. It didn't happen.

By the end of week three it was evident things were starting to fall apart for them. They were getting irritable and some serious bickering had begun. I surmised goodie withdrawal was playing a strong role in their cross dispositions as I hadn't baked their most-loved chocolate brownies or chocolate chip banana bread since the strike began.

Early into the fourth week I decided to test the waters by preparing a meal of grilled pork chops with chunky applesauce, steamed broccoli, garlic mashed potatoes and grilled corn-on-the-cob.

It had been a very long time since we enjoyed a meal so much.

Complaints from Brian and Holly were now replaced by lip smacking and the quiet savoring of a quality meal. Their dad and I hid our faces to cover the glow of parental triumph.

"That was a great supper! Thanks, Mom!" Both children bounced from their chairs when they were excused and dashed toward the sink to scrape, rinse and stack their plates. I even got a big hug from them as they were leaving the kitchen.

The kids understood that generous helpings of love and camaraderie are passed around a family dinner table. It just took some tough love for them to value the time and planning it takes in preparing meals, and to appreciate the challenges involved in pleasing everyone, not just one.

The cooking strike had served its purpose—the complaining came to a halt. The foods and meals I served thereafter received glowing reviews. And when they didn't like something, they were simply silent. They had learned!

~Cynthia Briggs

Getting to Know Jennifer

Tell me what you eat and I will tell what you are.
~Jean Anthelme Brillat-Savarin

The dark blue vinyl notebook on the kitchen bookshelf looks ordinary enough. Glancing through the three-ring binder, I note the neatly printed white tabs labeling the categories—appetizers, vegetables, seafood, poultry, meats, desserts, miscellaneous. They are written in Jennifer's neat printing, in blue ballpoint pen; this book speaks of an organized mind. The opening pale yellow page is splattered with a splotch of oil, so it appears to be well used. Some of the recipes, like the ever-popular Caramelized Brie, have been photocopied from newspaper clippings, while others, like Mozzarella Crostini, have been typed out on white paper. The calorie counts and serving sizes are dutifully noted at the bottom of each. So, I can conclude that Jennifer was a woman who liked cheese and counted calories. These facts seem to be contradictory.

There are handwritten notes, in Jennifer's big loopy script, noting the origin (*Miami Herald*, Mom, Mrs. Guilford, Kathy) of each recipe. So Jennifer was apparently a woman who cared about the origin of things. Pockets on the sides of the binder are stuffed with a variety of assorted recipes, in no particular order. These, I assume, were not the tried and true recipes in the main section, but recipes to be experimented with at a later date. Some were torn out of magazines (Grilled Lamb Chops from *Bon Appetit*), some handwritten on legal pad paper (Pasta Rustica) and some neatly cut off of packages (Indonesian Shrimp and Rice). Other recipes are from restaurants (Jalapeno Corn Bread) or grocery stores (Black Bean Chili) and some have handwritten notes attached.

"Jennifer, here is the recipe for the pound

cake that I promised you. Also, one of my favorites—Banana Supreme. It's easy to make and delicious if you like bananas and nuts." Did Jennifer like bananas and nuts? I wonder. And there are Creole recipes (Red Beans and Rice), which I know she collected because her husband loved Creole food.

I know this because her husband is now my husband. Jennifer died at thirty-nine of lung cancer, leaving behind three young daughters and a grieving husband named Zeke.

When I first started dating Zeke, there were pictures of Jennifer—a striking brunette with chiseled features and heavy bangs—around his house, as well as her books and the ceramic cats she collected. According to Zeke, she loved reading, cats and, more than anything else, her daughters. A tax attorney who chose to stay at home after her second daughter was born, Jennifer truly loved being a mom. She was also smart, getting a perfect score on her SATs, something I could never hope to do in a million years.

But Zeke sold his house, I sold mine and we bought a new house that would be "ours." The books and ceramic cats have been packed away, so what I am left with are these recipes in this blue vinyl binder; this everyday item that links me to my stepdaughters' mother and to my husband's deceased wife. I am reluctant to throw away any of the recipes she collected. What if it was a family favorite?

So I ask my husband if he remembers eating Pacific Rim Glazed Flank Steak or Greek Pizza. He does not. "What about Mahogany Beef Stew or Horseradish Mashed Potatoes?" I inquire. He shrugs with an apologetic look.

"Did Jennifer have any specialties she liked to cook?" I ask him as we walk around the block of our new house.

"She did make a good tuna curry," he offers. I remember the discussion of the curried tuna before. It was a recipe that Zeke first loved and then came to dread, as it made repeat appearances on a weekly basis. I look at the recipe: chopped onion, green pepper, butter, sour cream, curry powder and canned tuna, mixed together, baked and served over rice. I cannot in my wildest dreams imagine making this dish. Nor the one on the other side of the same sheet for African Chow Mein made with ground beef and rice. Yet, here's a recipe for Chili Cheese Soufflé that sounds interesting, and another for Mexican Chicken Strata that I have actually made many times. I wrote next to my recipe, clipped from the paper, "Everybody liked" in pencil. Of course, that was a different marriage, different husband, different life, and now with three little girls raised on pizza, pasta and chicken fingers, all bets are off with any recipe involving sourdough bread, black beans, and green chilies.

Looking at this collection of recipes, I feel an inexplicable sadness for the brief life of a woman I never even met. There's one for Bear Biscuits, complete with illustrations, on how to turn refrigerator biscuits, raisins and maraschino cherries into a smiling bear face.

I wonder if Jennifer ever got the chance to

make these with her daughters. They were only four, five and eight when she died. Mamma G's Meatloaf was a recipe passed down from Zeke's mother. I imagine Jennifer as a young bride mixing together the pork, beef and veal with sage, parsley and eggs to make her husband's favorite dinner in the hope it would please him. I have made the same meatloaf (as a not-so-young bride) with the same hope in mind.

And here's a collection of recipes printed off the Internet from The Barefoot Contessa, which promise "scrumptious party platters sure to sate even the most grinch-hearted guest" for the holidays. The five pages are stapled together and include recipes for Sun Dried Tomato Dip and Grilled Lemon Chicken with Satay Sauce. I look at the date it was printed—11/30/00. This was a year after she was diagnosed with cancer, two years before she died. "So," I think, "she was still planning on having dinner parties and entertaining." In the face of chemo and cancer, I admire her optimism and zest for life. She gathered these recipes because she planned to live, love and cook, despite the unlikely odds.

"Her Poppy Seed Torte was good too," Zeke adds, while we walk. I know this recipe as well. Zeke and I have attempted to make it together on two occasions. Each time we have gotten stuck at the same place and have had to call Jennifer's mother in California for clarification. Each time she has laughingly obliged and talked us through the recipe. I have made a note of it for whenever the third attempt may be.

So, I will make the Bear Biscuits with Jennifer's girls, who are now mine, I will make Mamma G's meatloaf to serve my family when they are in need of comfort and I will try out the Grilled Lemon Chicken with Satay Sauce in hopes that it will sate a Grinch-hearted guest. I will carry on the legacy and cook the foods that Jennifer cannot, because this is what we do. We carry on in the face of uncertainty, we put one foot in front of the other even when it doesn't feel possible and we plan dinner parties for the future because it gives us hope and happiness. And then we eat.

~Gina Lee Guilford

My Father's Famous Tuna Melt

Sometimes the poorest man leaves
his children the richest inheritance.
~Ruth E. Renkel

I can still remember the smell of hot tuna fresh out of the oven. I could be all the way up in my bedroom on the third floor of our old Victorian-style house and the odor would snake its way around corners, up three flights of stairs and to my bed where it would hover over me, jolting me from a sound sleep. I would be nauseated, on the verge of retching, covering my face with my pillow, but I just couldn't escape the fact that my father was making one of his famous, much-beloved tuna melts. Fresh white albacore with just the right amount of mayo, topped with an expertly browned piece of melted cheddar on a slice of toasted seeded rye. It was simple, but according to experts, it was perfection.

My father was as proud of his culinary creation as he was of his son winning a Little League trophy. His tuna melt was legendary. Friends and neighbors found any excuse to drop by on the off chance he would offer to make them one. And of course, he would rarely disappoint their eager palates. Everyone loved my father's tuna melt. That is, everyone but me.

The truth is, I never tried one. Not even a bite. I was just a kid and my taste buds demanded the simpler things in life—pizza, burgers, hot dogs. They were not sophisticated or daring enough to take a chance on hot fish covered in cheese.

My father pleaded with me through the years to give it a try. "Trust me," he would say, "you'll love it. Have I ever let you down before?" Truth is, he hadn't. His love guided me through my childhood, making sure I never had to worry about a thing. He taught me how to throw a baseball, patiently walked me through homework and spent countless hours teaching me about the world. Like many boys, I idolized my father. To me, his word was gospel.

But when it came to tuna melts, I would not budge. It pained me to disappoint this man who gave me everything, when all he was asking of me was to take a bite and share in his joy.

One day, when I was fifteen, after years of prodding and pleading, I finally agreed to give it a try. For him. I stood by his side in the kitchen as the ceremony began. He approached his ingredients like a surgeon approaching a patient in the operating room. He slowly pulled a long serrated knife from its wood block, expertly cutting a perfect slice through the warm loaf of rye. His control of the blade was masterful as he stabbed it into the waiting stick of butter and in one fluid motion slathered a generous amount all over the steaming bread. He opened the tuna can so fast you would have thought it was never sealed. He mixed the tuna and a perfectly rounded tablespoon of mayonnaise in a large bowl that gave him enough room to work his magic. His hands moved with lightning speed and precision as he put dollops of tuna onto the waiting bread. There was intense concentration in his eyes as he placed a slice of aged New York cheddar perfectly centered over his masterpiece. As a finishing touch, he sprinkled a dusting of paprika over the top. Sweat formed on his brow as he scooped up the entire creation and centered it in the pre-heated oven.

As the cheese began to bubble and brown, the corners bonding with the bread below, I could feel my father's excitement build at the thought of finally sharing the creation he loved with his only son. But as the bread began to toast and the cheese began to melt, the smell of the tuna as it began to heat up filled me with dread. I knew, at that moment, that I would never be able to do it.

I blamed it on a stomachache, running out

of the room before he even had a chance to remove it from the oven. And before I was able to see the look of disappointment on his face. That was the last tuna melt he ever made before he got sick.

As the cancer took its toll on his body, my father lost his appetite. As great as his will was, he could no longer do many of the things he loved: playing catch in the backyard, helping me with schoolwork, cooking. And he lost his ability to go through the painstaking steps necessary to create his tuna melt. Anything less than perfection would not be accepted. And surely the smell of hot tuna would not sit very well with him anymore.

What pained him more than not being able to eat his beloved tuna melts was not being able to make them for others and share in their joy and pleasure. Now neighbors and friends stopped by for a different reason.

My father had lost a lot of weight along with his appetite and could no longer leave his bed. I spent many nights lying next to him as he attempted to cram in all of life's lessons in the few weeks he had left. It was a long good-bye that went too quickly.

One night, as I sat by his side, he jolted up in bed with an energy I hadn't seen in months, uttering five simple words, "Make me a tuna melt."

Trying to be a dutiful son, I put aside my apprehension and ran to the kitchen. I felt unworthy as I stepped onto his stage. Laying the ingredients on the counter, I did my best to honor his ritualistic performance. I cut the bread. Slathered the butter. Mixed the tuna. Carefully placed the cheese. Sprinkled the paprika. I put it in the oven and watched it come to life. It was not the masterpiece my father spent years perfecting, but in my own way, I feel like I did him proud. As the bread toasted and the cheese melted, the smell of the heated tuna did not bother me as much.

I couldn't wait to see the look on his face as he took a bite of my first tuna melt. But as I brought it to him, though he tried to hide it, I could see him wince from the smell. He just couldn't do it. Dejected, I placed the plate on his night table and took a seat by his bedside. "Thank you," he said. Even through his nausea, he was beaming with pride. And for the first time, the smell of the melted cheese, toasted bread and even the warm tuna made my mouth water. I picked up the tuna melt, and took a bite. A smile crept over his face. He was right. It was delicious. He had never let me down.

My father died a few days later. He was way too young and so was I. But I still remember everything he taught me and try to live a life that would make him proud. To this day, I make my father's famous tuna melt once a week just the way he used to make it. And I don't even mind the smell anymore.

~David Chalfin

Cereal Killer

There is no sincerer love than the love of food.
~George Bernard Shaw

My friend Dominique and I are innkeepers at Channel Road Inn. Working at a bed and breakfast hotel is fun! We take reservations, help guests with their dinner plans and we bake homemade cookies, breakfast cakes and goodies from scratch every day for our guests.

Dominique and I have been friends for a while now. We've shared secrets, lots of laughs and even a few tears, but lately something has come between us ... it's her granola recipe. She won't tell me (or anyone!) how it's made.

Dominique's granola is the best thing I've ever tasted. Sure I love the homemade banana bread and blueberry cakes we bake at the Inn. Our scones, egg soufflés and French toast are amazing and our homemade chocolate chip cookies are to die for but nothing—NOTH-ING!—can top Dominique's granola.

When you ask Dominique what's in the granola she pretends to tell you. "Oh, it's simple—just your basic granola but I add in some fruit and I sweeten it with coconut and honey," she says (while not looking you in the eye). But she must be leaving something out of her description because I have never tasted granola (or anything) that tastes as good as this. I cannot even hear, much less talk, when I'm eating this granola. The whole world stops moving and all I can hear is the crunching of the granola in my mouth. I can't hear the phones or the doorbell ring and even when people talk to me, I can see their lips moving but their voices sound like they are in slow motion. In that sense, Dominique's granola is an occupational hazard for me, so I try to eat it only after my shift has ended.

I am known to get overly exuberant about certain things, so I took a sample of

Dominique's granola to one of my girlfriends at Curves so she could tell me if she found it as amazing as I do. By the time I drove home, there was already an e-mail from my girlfriend saying, "Wow, you were not kidding! That stuff is addictive! Yum, yum, yum! I'm thinking Dominique should start small and go to farmers' markets, fairs, etc. ... and just sell locally ... word will spread!"

And word has spread! Though Dominique has not had time to go to farmers' markets or fairs yet, we do have guests e-mailing and calling to ask for the recipe for Dominique's homemade granola. Over the past twenty-three years all of the innkeepers at Channel Road Inn have been open and generous with our recipes. We freely and willingly give them to our guests and we'll even let them watch us bake the cakes or prepare the egg soufflés and French toast so they can replicate them at home. Dominique's granola is the only recipe they cannot have. Their response is always the same. They laugh and say, "I always knew you

innkeepers had a few tricks up your sleeves,"
and then they add, "No problem. But can I buy
some of that granola? Could you mail it to me?
I keep thinking about it."

I like these phone calls and e-mails because
they reassure me that I have not lost my mind.
This granola is that good! I think about it every
day and always hope Dominique has had a
chance to make it when I come into work. I've
even been known to call down to the Inn on
my days off just to see if, by chance, Domi has
made any granola. I scour the freezer at the Inn
looking for leftovers and hidden stashes, but I
rarely find any because the guests eat it by the
heaping spoonfuls. On the days Dominique's
granola gets served, our homemade cakes are
barely touched. People are nuts for this stuff.

My girlfriend from Curves asks me on a
weekly basis how she can get more of
Dominique's granola. Though she has an
apartment nearby, she's considering booking
a room at Channel Road Inn just so she can
come to breakfast and eat granola. It's that

bad—this granola is ruining the lives of everyone who eats it. We all become addicts and start devoting our lives to finding out how and when we can get more granola.

And all the while, Dominique sits in the kitchen feigning surprise that everyone is rabidly searching for more granola. She's like the Master of the Universe—the one who holds the key to our happiness. When she knows I'm having a hard week, she definitely makes granola. One time she even went out and bought coconut herself because the Inn was out of it and she knew I wanted and needed (yes, actually needed) her homemade granola that day.

We have a repeat guest at Channel Road Inn who has stayed at the Inn several times a year for the past ten years. She's crazy about Dominique's granola too! Like me, she has begged for the recipe and then finally settled for just eating a bowl of granola once she realized that Dominique's vague description of "fruit, coconut and honey" is just a dodge. We all adore this guest—from her Missouri drawl to her darling grandchildren and impeccable manners, she is the most charming woman in the world.

Under normal circumstances, there's nothing I would deny this guest, but when she checked in last week and immediately asked if "Dominique had made any granola" I had to think fast. The technical answer was, "No, Domi has not had time to make granola today." But the underlying truth, the one that troubled my heart was, "Domi has not had time to make granola today ... but she did give me a small bag of it last week. I have it hidden in the back of the freezer with my name on it and I have been rationing it out to myself half a cup at a time."

I stared at our loyal guest, wondering if I should share my secret stash with her. I love this guest... but I also love Dominique's granola. I adore this guest... but I also adore Dominique's granola. I should have shared my granola with this guest... but I didn't. I tried to ease my conscience by offering her a cup of tea and a slice of hot vanilla streusel cake, fresh out of the oven. She politely said, "No thank you" and as I watched her walk down the hall to her room, I felt slightly bad—but not as bad as I would have felt had I given her the last of my granola.

Dominique shows her love for Channel Road Inn's guests—and employees—through her baking. She works on her recipes for weeks to perfect them and is truly delighted when the guests "ooh and ah" over her creations. She is generous with most of her recipes, except for one. And that's okay, because this granola is so good, I'm betting one day it will be available in stores, and then our charming guest from Missouri, my girlfriend from Curves, and I can all eat Domi's granola to our heart's content!

~Rebecca Hill

Meet Our Contributors

Barbara Blossom Ashmun gardens on an acre in Portland, OR. She's written six garden books, most recently *Married to My Garden*, about her love affair with plants. A garden columnist for the *Portland Tribune* since 2004, she's also contributed to magazines and anthologies. She blogs at blessings fromthegarden.blogspot.com.

Cynthia Briggs embraces her love of cooking and writing through her story-filled cookbooks *Pork Chops & Applesauce* and *Sweet Apple Temptations*. She enjoys speaking to women's groups, critiquing and reviewing books, and writing for various publications. Coaching budding authors is her most recent passion. E-mail Cynthia at info@porkchopsandapplesauce.net.

David Chalfin is a native New Yorker living in Los Angeles as a television and film editor. He received his B.A. from the University of Pennsylvania and an M.A. in Media Studies from The New School. He lives for a good slice of NY pizza. E-mail him at dchalf@aol.com.

Beverly Golberg, of St. Paul, MN, began writing after retirement from paralegal work. Her essays have appeared in the literary journals *ARS Medica* and *Willard & Maple*, *Cottage Life* magazine, the St. Paul *Pioneer Press*, and various anthologies. She reads her work at the Wild Yam Cabaret in St. Paul.

Gina Guilford received her master's degree in Screenwriting at University of Miami in 2003. She has published articles in national magazines and has written an original sitcom based on her blended family. Her screenplay, *The Sweet Spot*, won various awards, including first place in All She Wrote. Learn more at gleesganders.blogspot.com.

Rebecca Hill and Tom Caufield live in Los Angeles. She and her friend Dominique work at Channel Road Inn and the Inn at Playa del Rey. Rebecca's stories have appeared in previous *Chicken Soup for the Soul* anthologies and in *Redbook* magazine. Her novel is entitled *Confessions of an Innkeeper*.

Mary Potter Kenyon cooks up soup and words in the Manchester, Iowa home she shares with her husband David and four of their eight children. Her writing appears in magazines, anthologies and the local newspaper. She is working with her agent on a book about couponing and blogs at marypotterkenyon.wordpress.com.

Linda O'Connell teaches in St. Louis, MO. Her humorous and inspirational essays have been published in twelve *Chicken Soup for the Soul* titles and many other regional and national publications. When Linda is wrist-deep in flour and sugar, she is knee-deep in thought. Linda blogs at lindaocon nell.blogspot.com.

Linda St.Cyr is a writer, blogger, activist, and short story author. When she isn't writing or raising her kids with her life partner, she is busy being vocal about feeding the hungry, sheltering the homeless, and bringing attention to human rights violations all over the world.

Diane Stark is a former elementary school teacher turned stay-at-home mom and freelance writer. She is a frequent contributor to the *Chicken Soup for the Soul* series. She is the author of *Teachers' Devotions to Go*. E-mail her at Diane Stark19@yahoo.com.

Linda C. Wright is an award-winning freelance writer and lives in Viera, FL. She's had many of her personal stories anthologized. Linda enjoys traveling, reading and photography. She is working on her second novel. E-mail her at lindacwright@ymail.com.

Meet Our Authors

Jack Canfield is the co-creator of the *Chicken Soup for the Soul* series, which *Time* magazine has called "the publishing phenomenon of the decade." Jack is also the coauthor of many other bestselling books.

Jack is the CEO of the Canfield Training Group in Santa Barbara, California, and founder of the Foundation for Self-Esteem in Culver City, California. He has conducted intensive personal and professional development seminars on the principles of success for more than a million people in twenty-three countries, has spoken to hundreds of thousands of people at more than 1,000 corporations, universities, professional conferences and conventions, and has been seen by millions more on national television shows.

Jack has received many awards and honors, including three honorary doctorates and a Guinness World Records Certificate for having seven books from the *Chicken Soup for the Soul* series appearing on the *New York Times* bestseller list on May 24, 1998.

You can reach Jack at
www.jackcanfield.com.

Mark Victor Hansen is the co-founder of Chicken Soup for the Soul, along with Jack Canfield. He is a sought-after keynote speaker, bestselling author, and marketing maven. Mark's powerful messages of possibility, opportunity, and action have created powerful change in thousands of organizations and millions of individuals worldwide.

Mark is a prolific writer with many bestselling books in addition to the *Chicken Soup for the Soul* series. Mark has had a profound influence in the field of human potential through his library of audios, videos, and articles in the areas of big thinking, sales achievement, wealth building, publishing success, and personal and professional development. He is also the founder of the MEGA Seminar Series.

Mark has received numerous awards that honor his entrepreneurial spirit, philanthropic heart, and business acumen. He is a lifetime member of the Horatio Alger Association of Distinguished Americans.

You can reach Mark at
www.markvictorhansen.com.

Amy Newmark is Chicken Soup for the Soul's publisher and editor-in-chief, after a thirty-year career as a writer, speaker, financial analyst, and business executive in the worlds of finance and telecommunications. Amy is a *magna cum laude* graduate of Harvard College, where she majored in Portuguese, minored in French, and traveled extensively. She and her husband have four grown children.

After a long career writing books on telecommunications, voluminous financial reports, business plans, and corporate press releases, Chicken Soup for the Soul is a breath of fresh air for Amy. She has fallen in love with Chicken Soup for the Soul and its life-changing books, and really enjoys putting these books together for Chicken Soup for the Soul's wonderful readers. She has coauthored more than five dozen *Chicken Soup for the Soul* books and has edited another three dozen.

You can reach Amy with any questions or comments through webmaster@chickensoupforthesoul.com and you can follow her on Twitter @amynewmark or @chickensoupsoul.

Chicken Soup for the Soul
Improving Your Life Every Day

Real people sharing real stories—for twenty years. Now, Chicken Soup for the Soul has gone beyond the bookstore to become a world leader in life improvement. Through books, movies, DVDs, online resources and other partnerships, we bring hope, courage, inspiration and love to hundreds of millions of people around the world. Chicken Soup for the Soul's writers and readers belong to a one-of-a-kind global community, sharing advice, support, guidance, comfort, and knowledge.

Chicken Soup for the Soul stories have been translated into more than forty languages and can be found in more than one hundred countries. Every day, millions of people experience a Chicken Soup for the Soul story in a book, magazine, newspaper or online. As we share our life experiences through these stories, we offer hope, comfort and inspiration to one another. The stories travel from person to person, and from country to country, helping to improve lives everywhere.

Share with Us

We all have had Chicken Soup for the Soul moments in our lives. If you would like to share your story or poem with millions of people around the world, go to chickensoup.com and click on "Submit Your Story." You may be able to help another reader, and become a published author at the same time. Some of our past contributors have launched writing and speaking careers from the publication of their stories in our books!

Our submission volume has been increasing steadily—the quality and quantity of your submissions has been fabulous. We only accept story submissions via our website. They are no longer accepted via mail or fax.

To contact us regarding other matters, please e-mail webmaster@chickensoupforthesoul.com, or fax or write us at:

Chicken Soup for the Soul
P.O. Box 700
Cos Cob, CT 06807-0700
Fax: 203-861-7194

One more note from your friends at Chicken Soup for the Soul: Occasionally, we receive an unsolicited book manuscript from one of our readers, and we would like to respectfully inform you that we do not accept unsolicited manuscripts and we must discard the ones that appear.